TODAY'S HITS

T0039462

ISBN: 978-1-5400-2908-9

HAL•LEONARD®

Visit Hal Leonard Online at
www.halleonard.com

Contact Us:
Hal Leonard
7777 West Bluemound Road
Milwaukee, WI 53213
Email: info@halleonard.com

In Europe contact:
Hal Leonard Europe Limited
Distribution Centre, Newmarket Road
Bury St Edmunds, Suffolk, IP33 3YB
Email: info@halleonardeurope.com

In Australia contact:
Hal Leonard Australia Pty. Ltd.
4 Lentara Court
Cheltenham, Victoria, 3192 Australia
Email: info@halleonard.com.au

CONTENTS

Believer

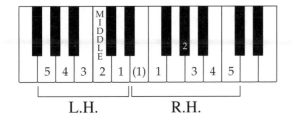

Words and Music by Dan Reynolds,
Wayne Sermon, Ben McKee, Daniel Platzman,
Justin Trantor, Mattias Larsson
and Robin Fredricksson

Moderate Rock Shuffle

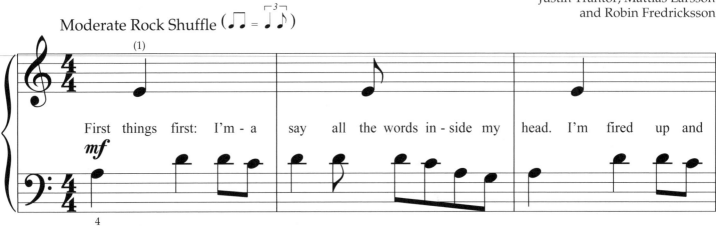

First things first: I'm-a say all the words in-side my head. I'm fired up and

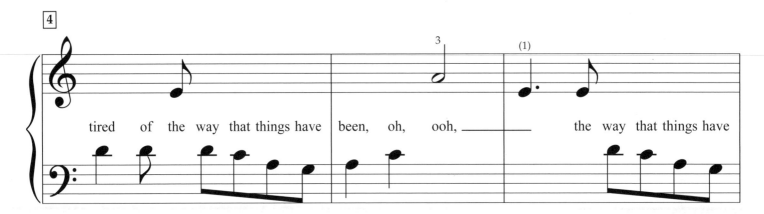

tired of the way that things have been, oh, ooh, _____ the way that things have

Duet Part (Student plays one octave higher than written.)

Moderate Rock Shuffle

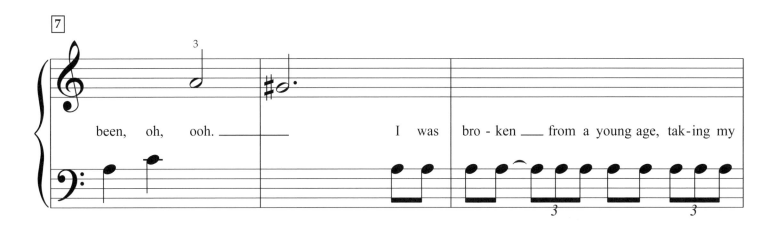

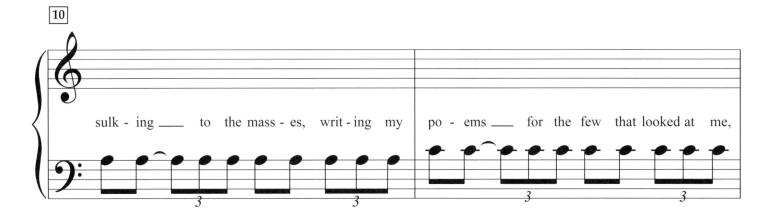

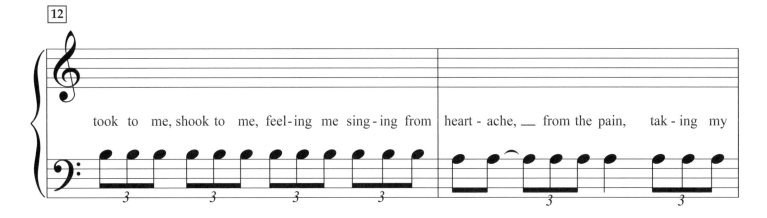

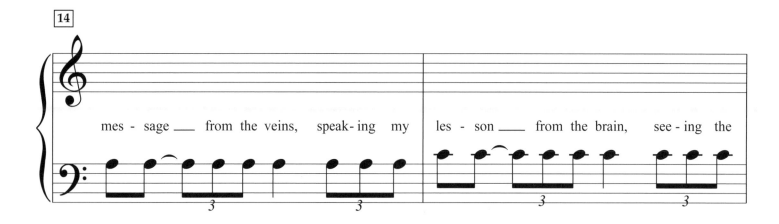

mes - sage ___ from the veins, speak-ing my | les - son ___ from the brain, see - ing the

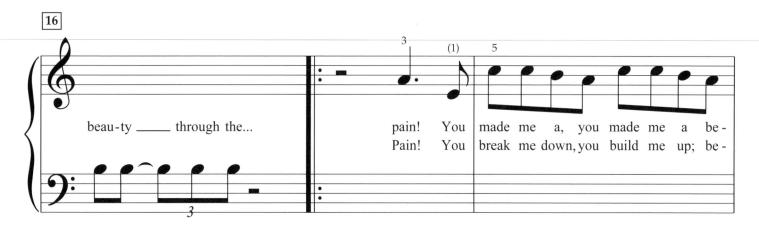

beau-ty ___ through the... | pain! You | made me a, you made me a be-
Pain! You | break me down, you build me up; be-

liev - er, be - liev - er. | Pain! ___ Oh,
liev - er, be - liev - er.

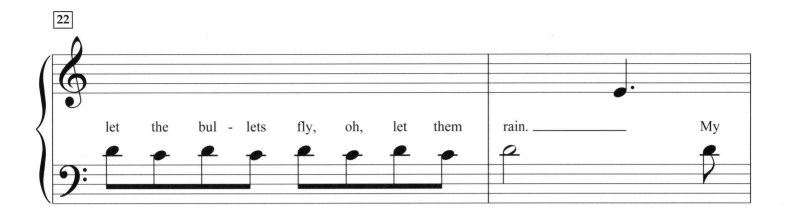

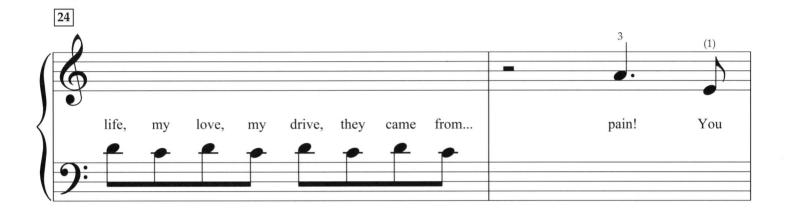

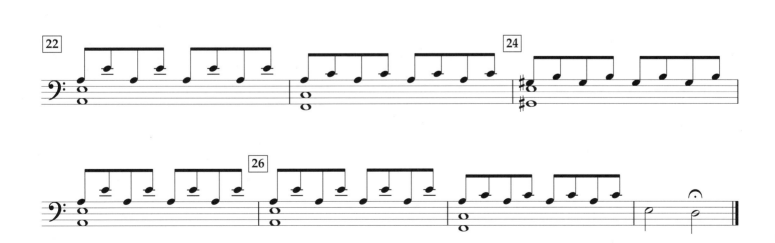

Best Day of My Life

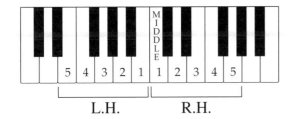

L.H.   R.H.

Words and Music by Zachary Barnett,
James Adam Shelley, Matthew Sanchez,
David Rublin, Shep Goodman
and Aaron Accetta

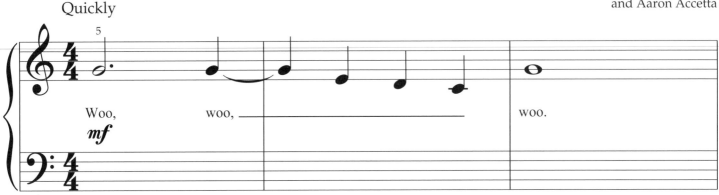

Woo,   woo, _____   woo.

I
had a dream so   big and loud, _ I
stretched my hands out to the sky, _ we

Duet Part (Student plays one octave higher than written.)

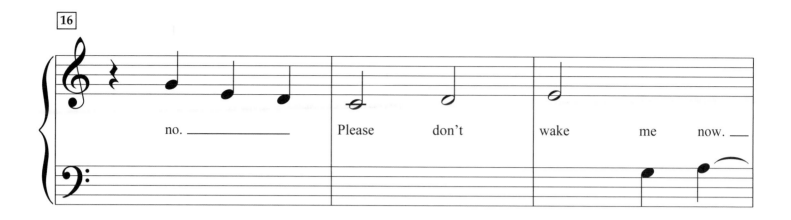

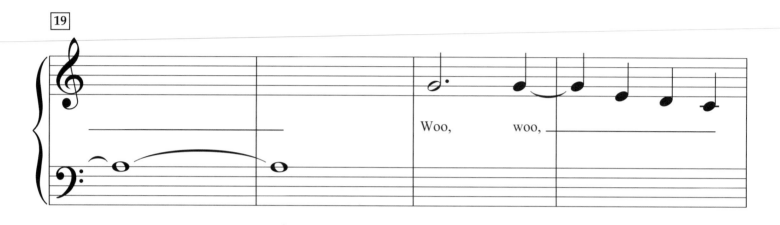

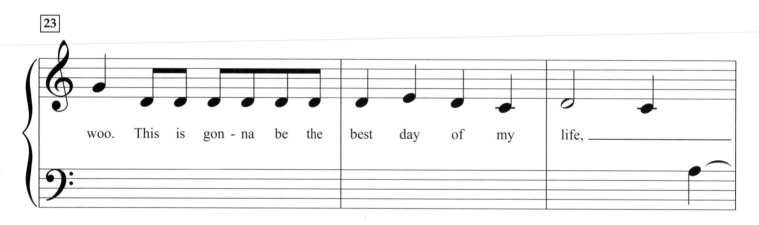

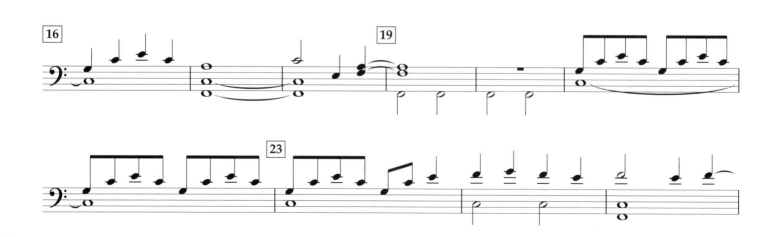

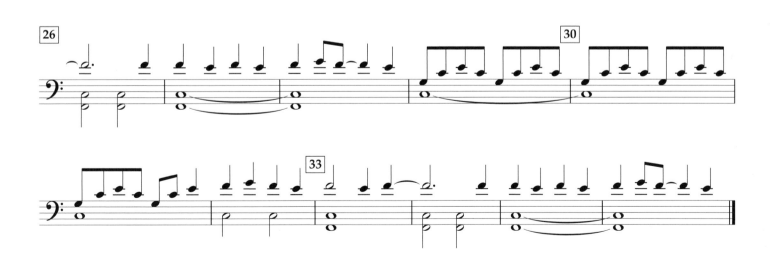

Brave

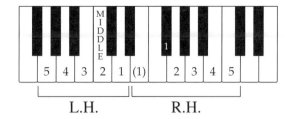

Words and Music by Sara Bareilles
and Jack Antonoff

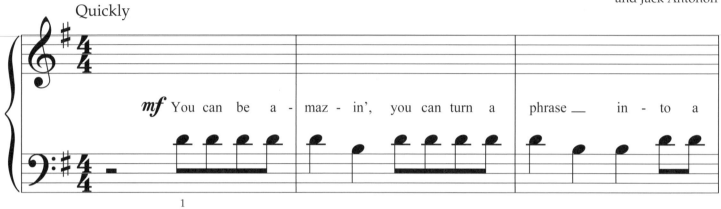

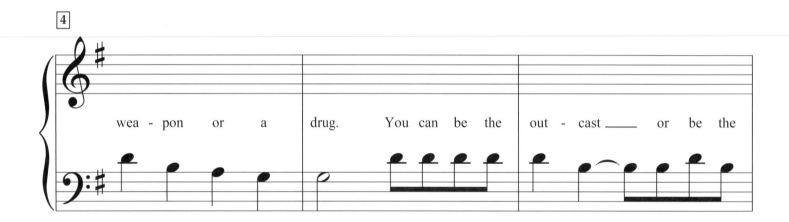

Duet Part (Student plays one octave higher than written.)

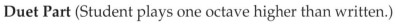

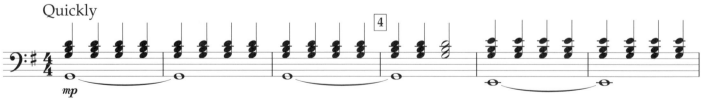

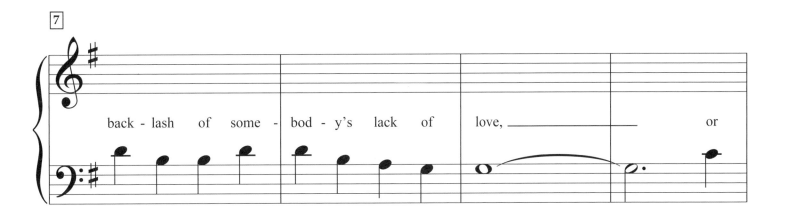

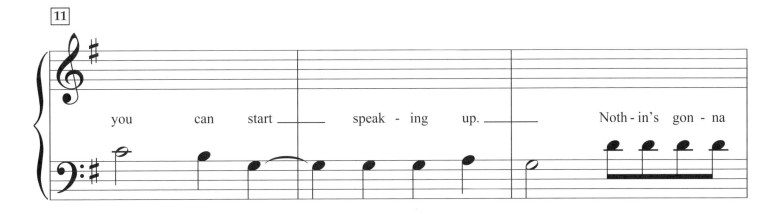

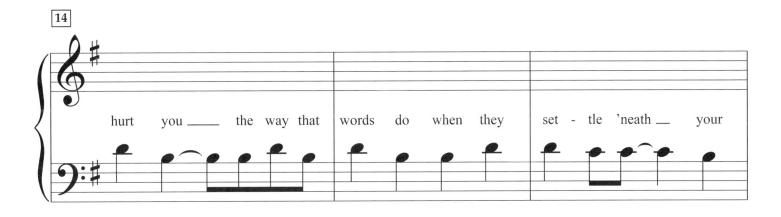

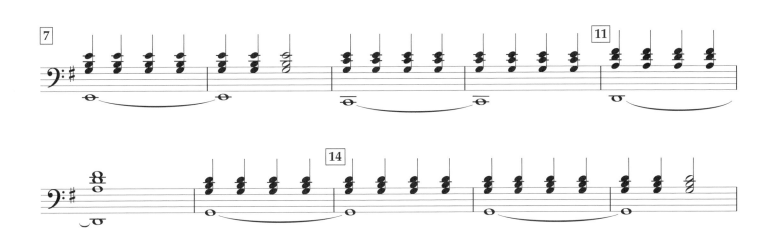

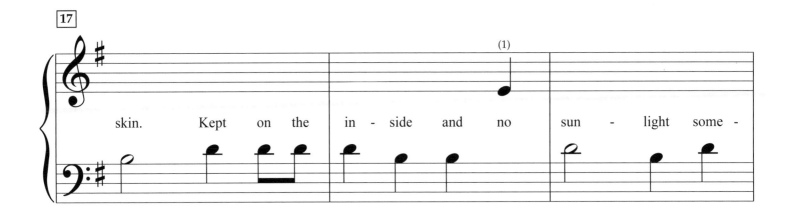

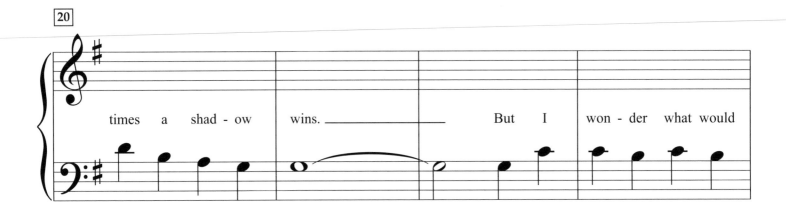

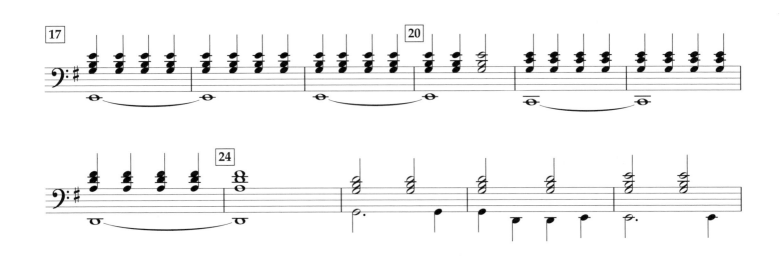

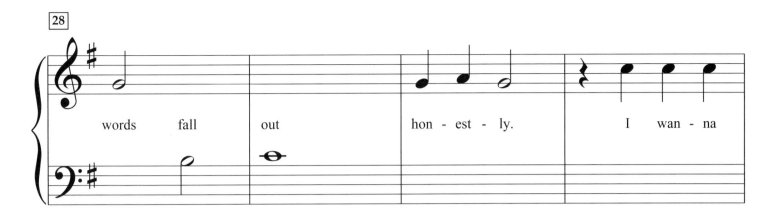

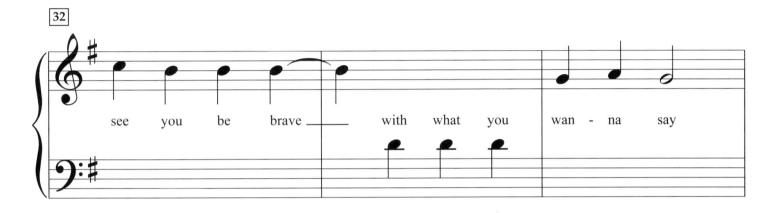

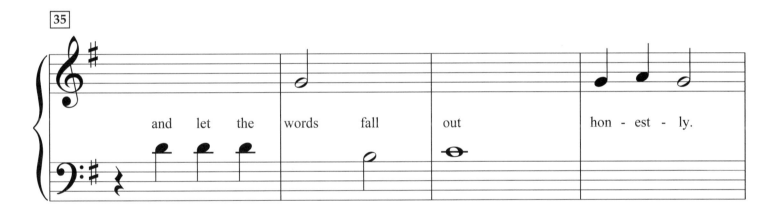

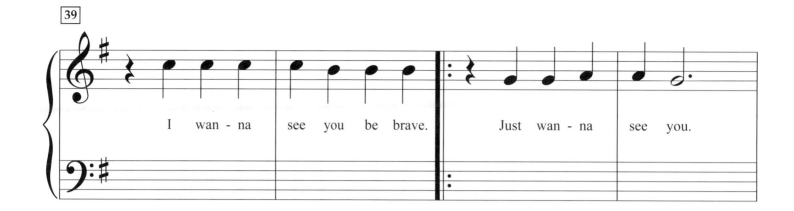

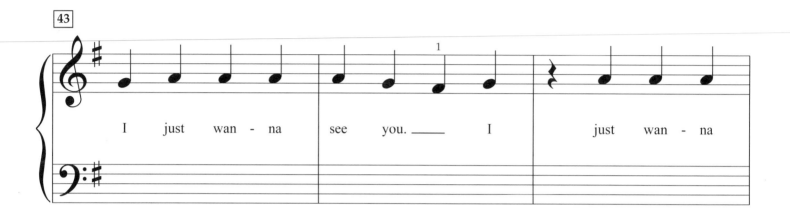

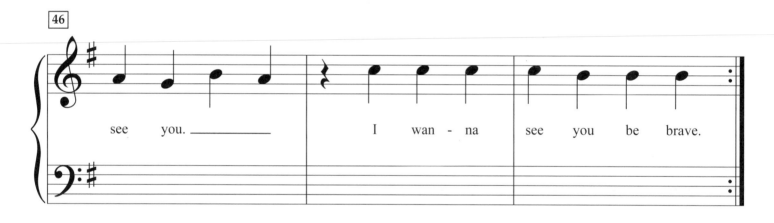

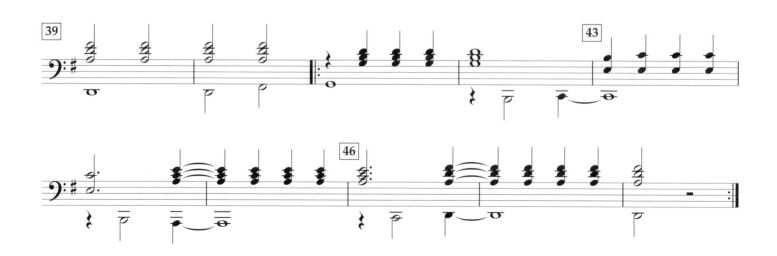

Perfect

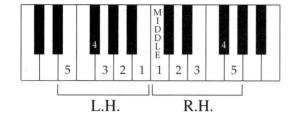

Words and Music by
Ed Sheeran

Moderately

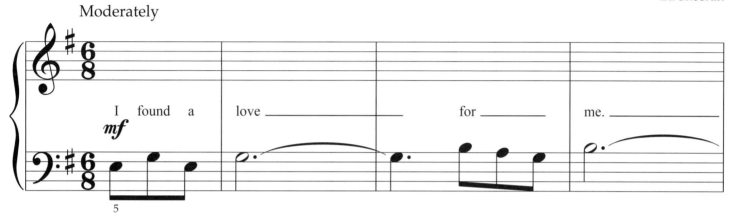

I found a love for me.

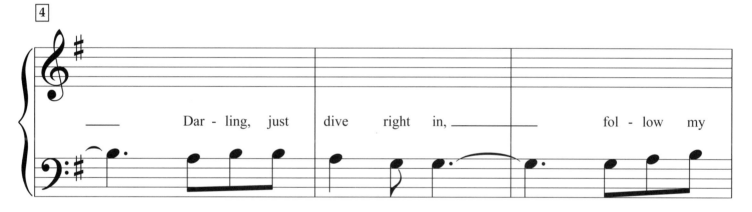

Dar - ling, just dive right in, fol - low my

Duet Part (Student plays one octave higher than written.)

Moderately

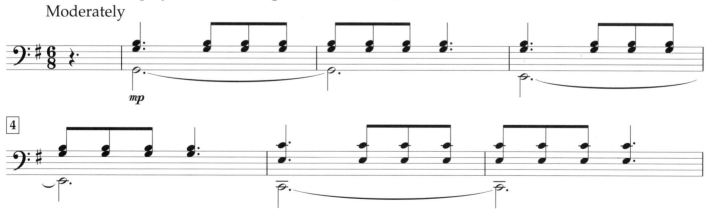

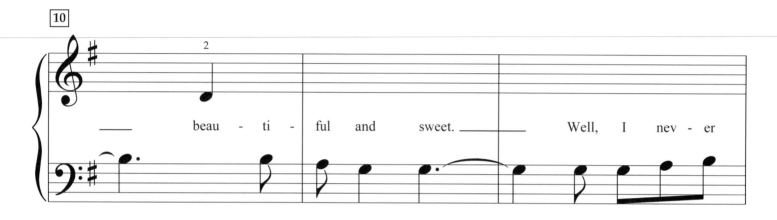

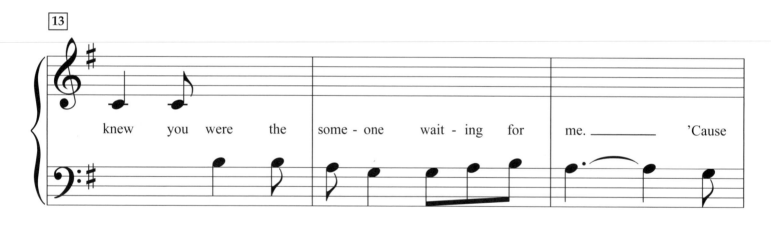

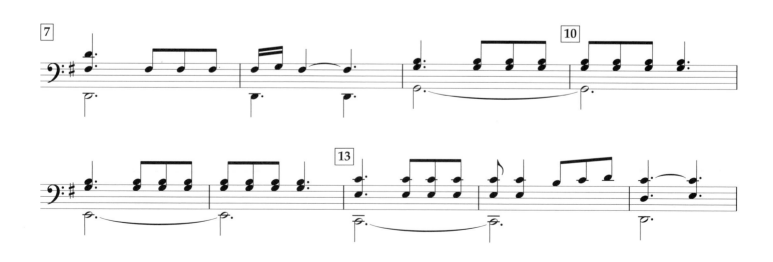

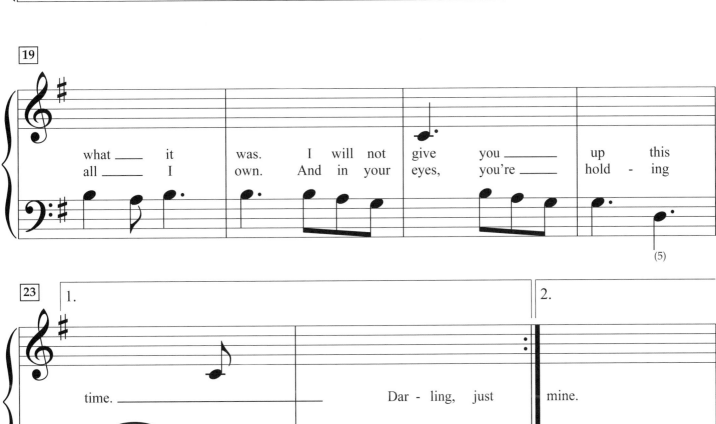

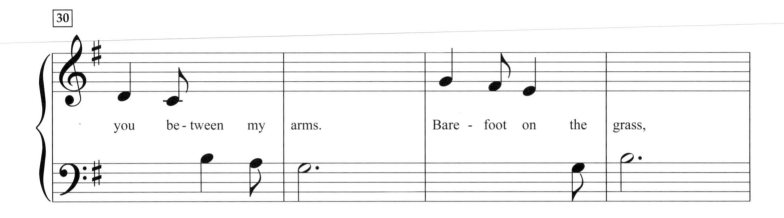

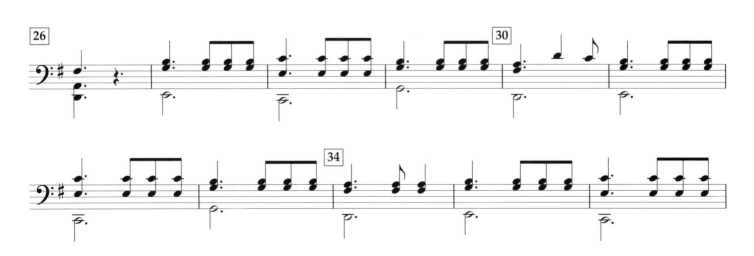

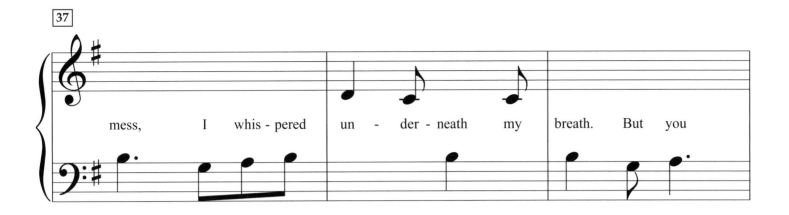

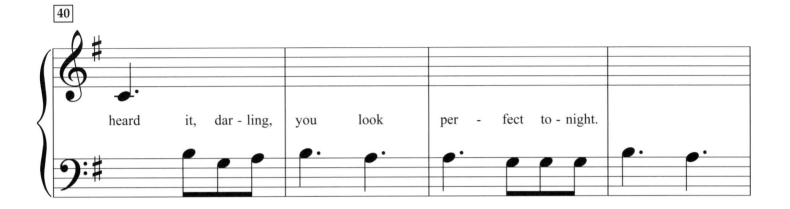

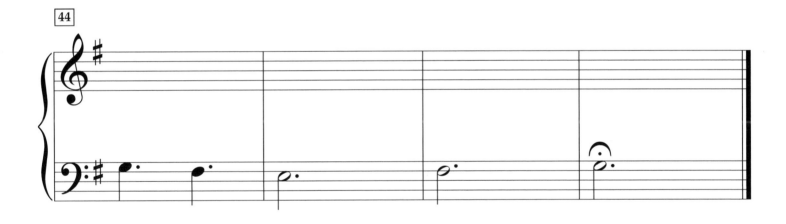

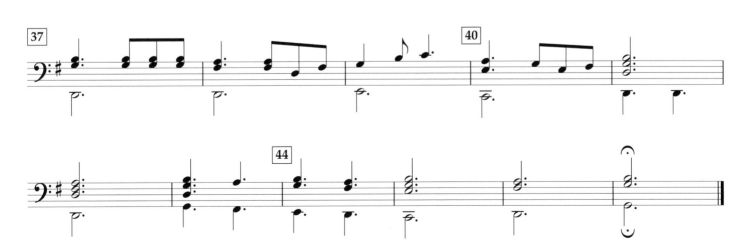

City of Stars
from LA LA LAND

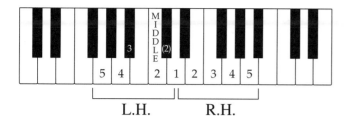

Music by Justin Hurwitz
Lyrics by Benj Pasek & Justin Paul

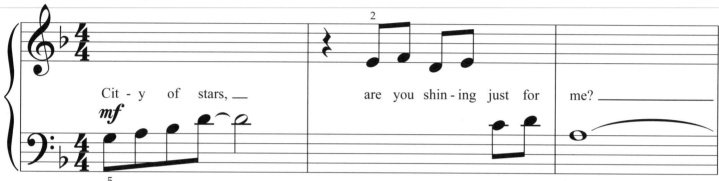

Cit - y of stars, —— are you shin - ing just for me? ——————

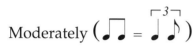

—— Cit - y of stars, —— there's so much that I can't

Duet Part (Student plays one octave higher than written.)

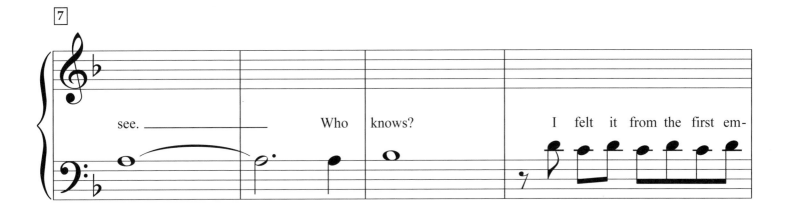

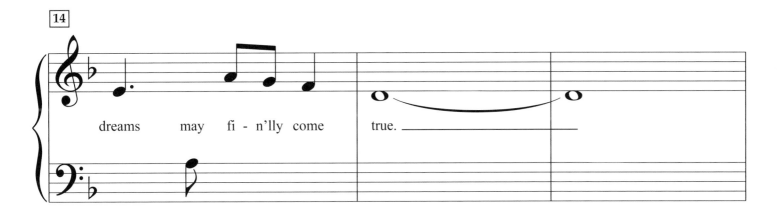

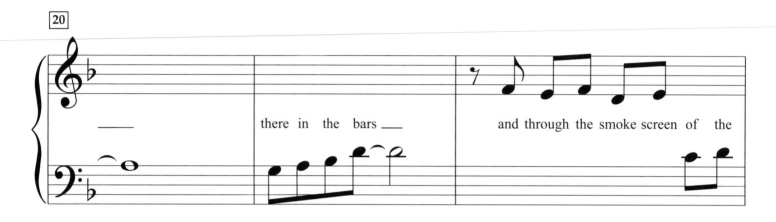

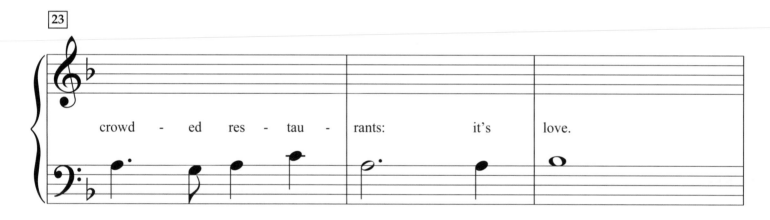

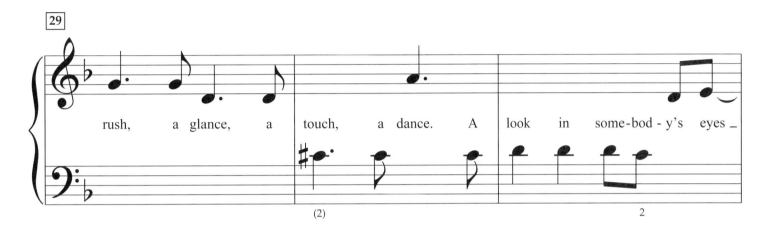

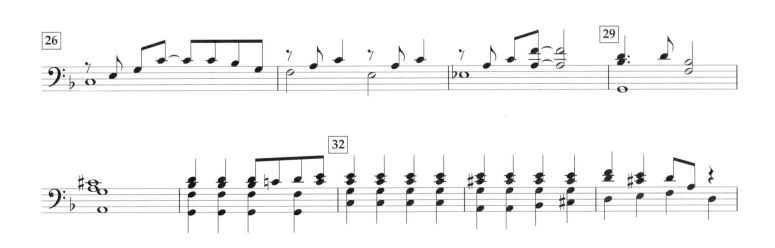

voice that says, "I'll be here, ____ and you'll be al - right." _____

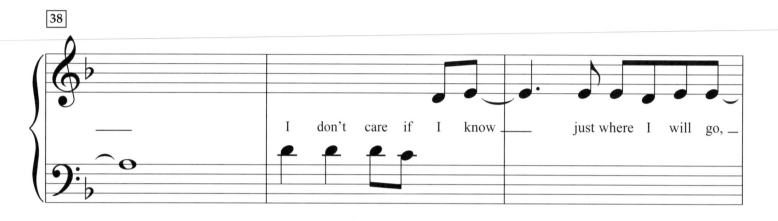

____ I don't care if I know ____ just where I will go, __

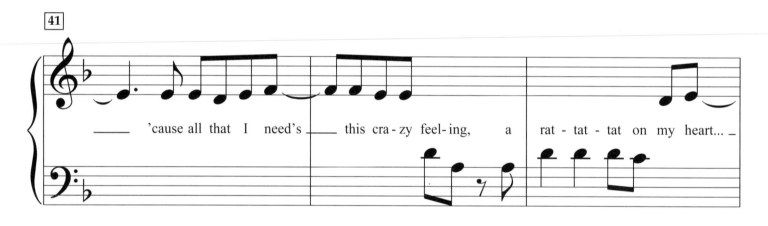

____ 'cause all that I need's ____ this cra - zy feel-ing, a rat - tat - tat on my heart... _

Think I want it to stay. ———

(2)

Cit - y of stars, ——   are you shin-ing just for   me? ———

2

Cit - y of stars, ——   you nev - er shined so   bright - ly. ———

(2)

One Call Away

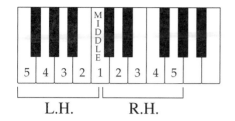

Words and Music by Charlie Puth,
Breyan Isaac, Matt Prime,
Justin Franks, Blake Anthony Carter
and Maureen McDonald

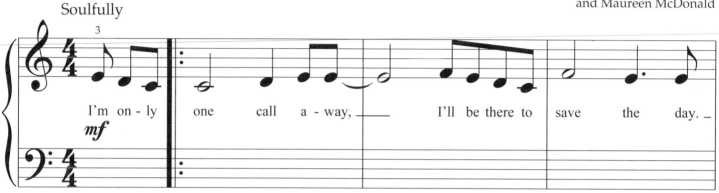

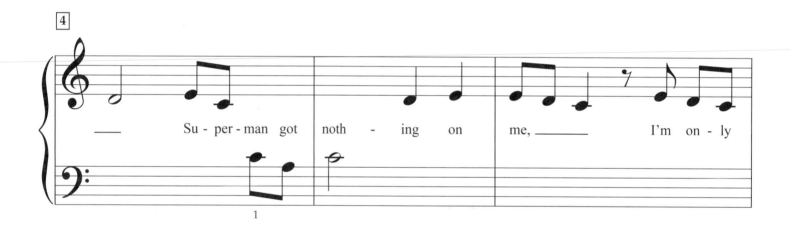

Duet Part (Student plays one octave higher than written.)

Soulfully

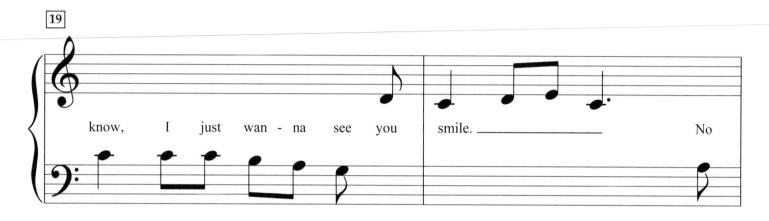

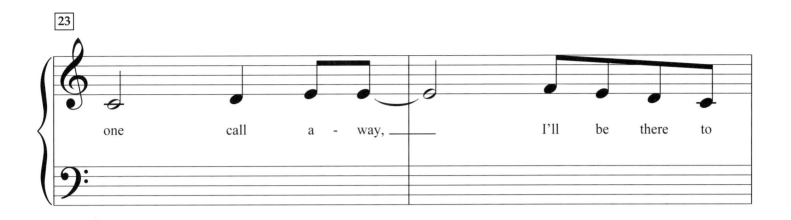

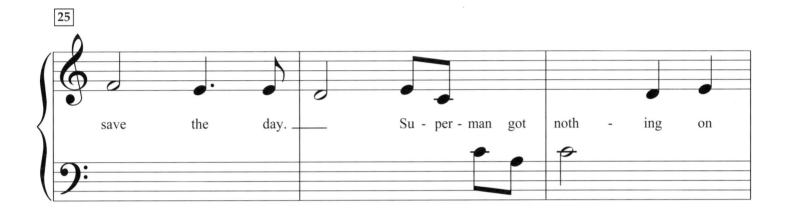

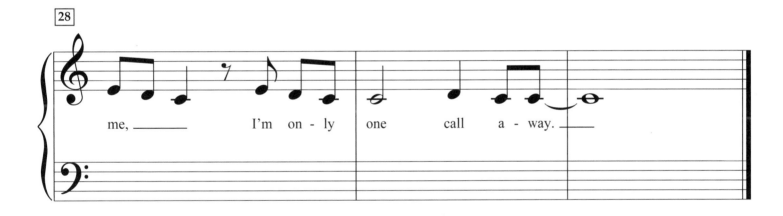

A Sky Full of Stars

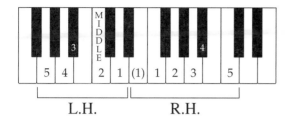

Words and Music by Guy Berryman,
Jon Buckland, Will Champion,
Chris Martin and Tim Bergling

Moderate Dance groove

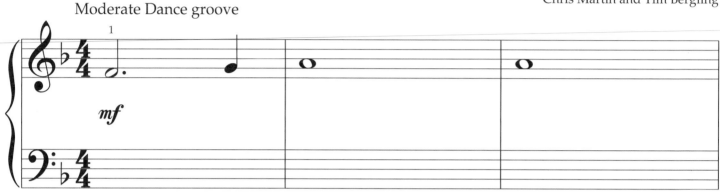

'Cause you're a sky, _____ 'cause you're a
'Cause you're a sky, _____ 'cause you're a

Duet Part (Student plays one octave higher than written.)

Moderate Dance groove

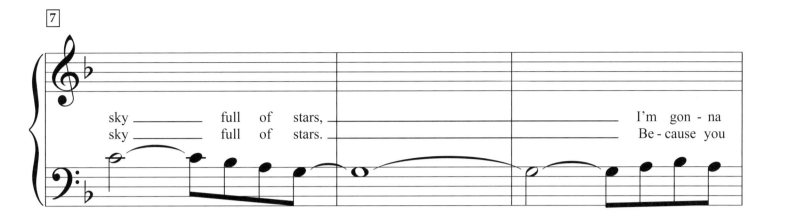

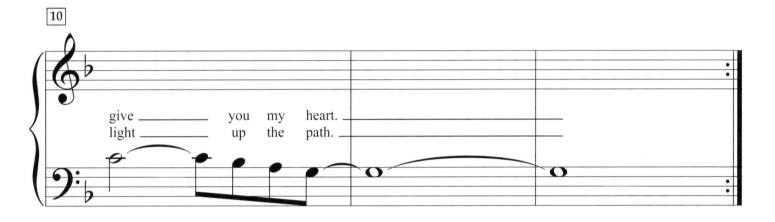

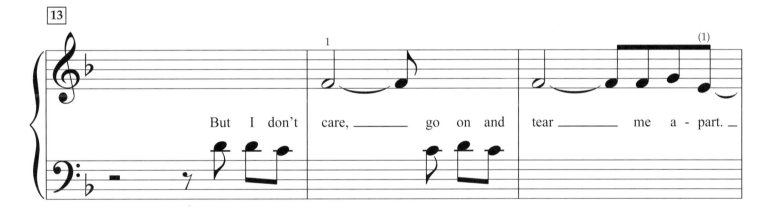

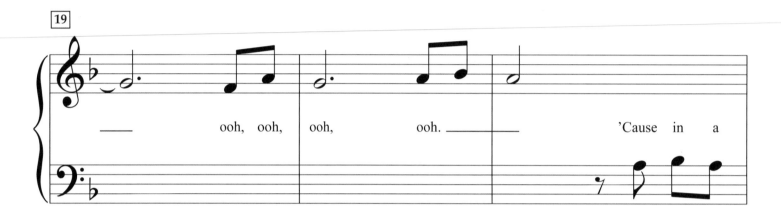

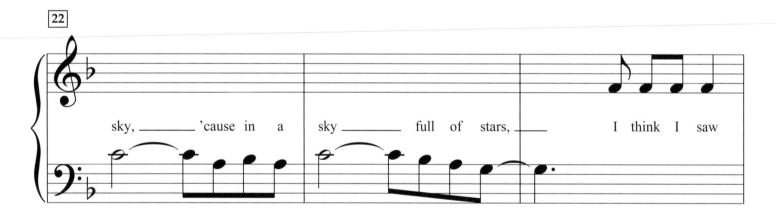

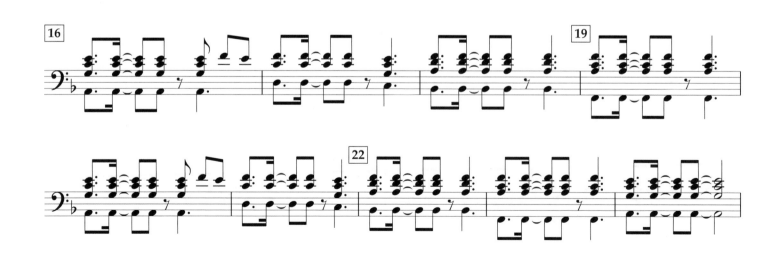

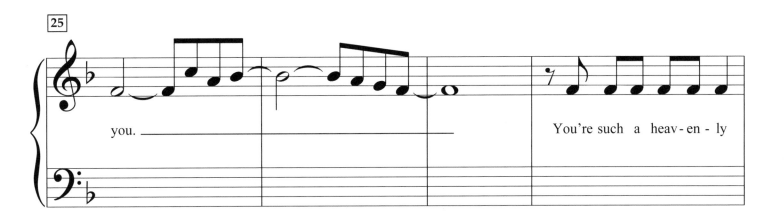

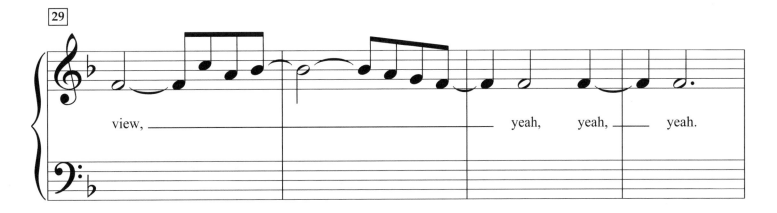

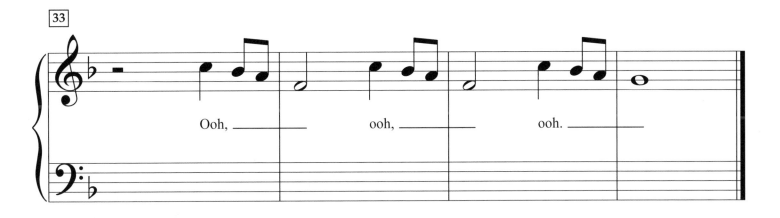

What About Us

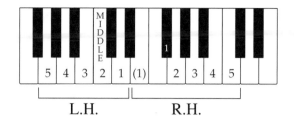

Words and Music by Alecia Moore,
Steve Mac and Johnny McDaid

Moderately

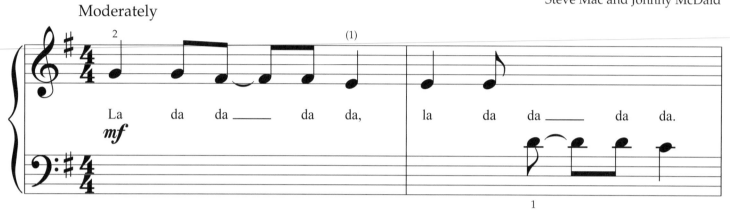

La da da ____ da da, la da da ____ da da.

mf

Da da da ____ da da. ____ We are

Duet Part (Student plays one octave higher than written.)

Moderately

mp

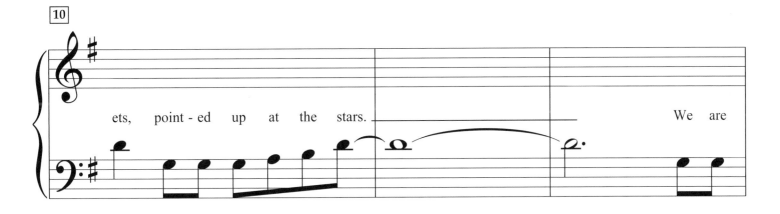

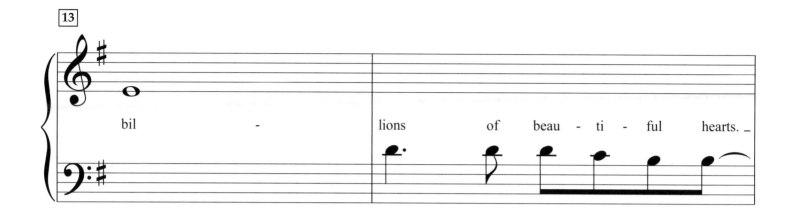

bil - lions of beau - ti - ful hearts. _

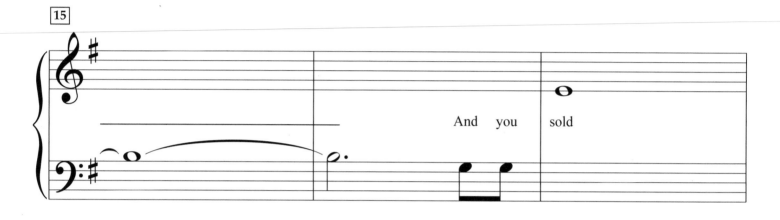

And you sold

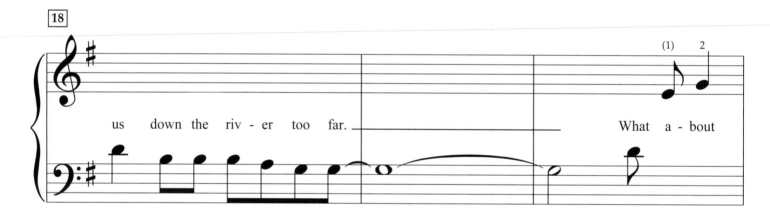

us down the riv - er too far. _ What a - bout

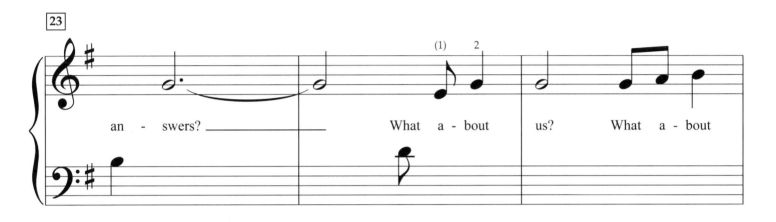

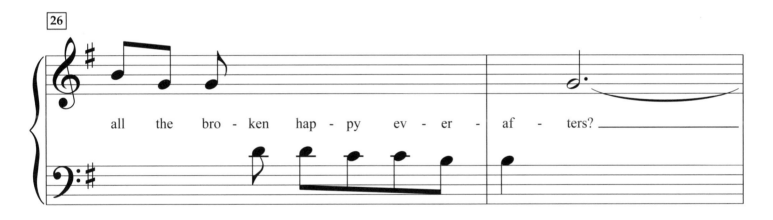

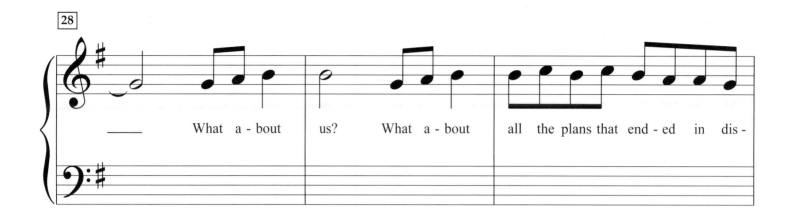

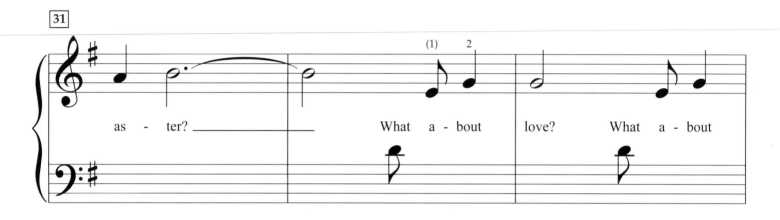

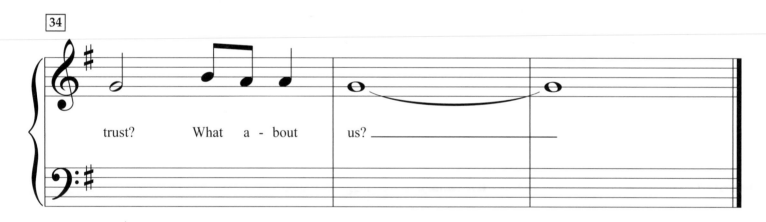